for

VIOLA

with piano accompaniment

By HARVEY S. WHISTLER and HERMAN A. HUMMEL

Contents

Adagio

from the Moonlight Sonata

VIOLA

L. van BEETHOVEN
Edited by Harvey S. Whistler
Arr. by Herman A. Hummel

Bourrée

from the Sixth Sonata

VIOLA

G. F. HANDEL

Edited by Harvey S. Whistler

Arr. by Herman A. Hummel

Allegro con spirito

Jeanie With the Light Brown Hair

VIOLA

STEPHEN C. FOSTER
Arr. by Herman A. Hummel

Edited by Harvey S. Whistler

Andante cantabile

None But the Lonely Heart

VIOLA

P. I. TSCHAIKOWSKY
Arr. by Herman A. Hummel

Edited by Harvey S. Whistler

Reverie

VIOLA

CLAUDE DEBUSSY

Edited by Harvey S. Whistler

Arr. by Herman A. Hummel

Pavane

(Pavane pour une Infante Défunte)

VIOLA

MAURICE RAVEL

Edited by Harvey S. Whistler

Arr. by Herman A. Hummel

The Holy City

VIOLA

Edited by Harvey S. Whistler

STEPHEN ADAMS

Arr. by Herman A. Hummel

Panis Angelicus

from the Messe Solennelle

VIOLA

CÉSAR FRANCK

Arr. by Herman A. Hummel

Edited by Harvey S. Whistler

Andächtig

Musette

from the Second Classical Suite

VIOLA

JEAN-MARIE LECLAIR
Arr. by Herman A. Hummel

Edited by Harvey S. Whistler

Rondo alla Zingaresa

VIOLA

HENRI ERNST

Arr. by Herman A. Hummel

Edited by Harvey S. Whistler

Brillante e con anima

f

Air Varié de Concert

VIOLA

CHAS. DANCLA

Edited by Harvey S. Whistler

Arr. by Herman A. Hummel

* The accompanying tones are plucked with the third or fourth finger of the left hand, while the bow sustains the melody.

Theme and Variations

VIOLA

Edited by Harvey S. Whistler

CHAS. de BERIOT
Arr. by Herman A. Hummel

VARIATION X
VARIATION XI
VARIATION XII
FINALE
spiccato sempre
cresc.
IIIp.
Ip.
FR

Sabre Dance

from the Gayne Ballet

VIOLA

ARAM KHACHATURIAN
Arr. by Herman A. Hummel

Edited by Harvey S. Whistler